Where is the baby?

Shelley Davidow

MACMILLAN
CARIBBEAN

Today is Saturday.
Mother is going to the clinic.
She is a nurse.

Grandmother is going to the shops.
She wants to buy a
new pillow.

Sam is sweeping the yard.
Alice is watering the plants.
Where is the baby?

They see Alice's friends.

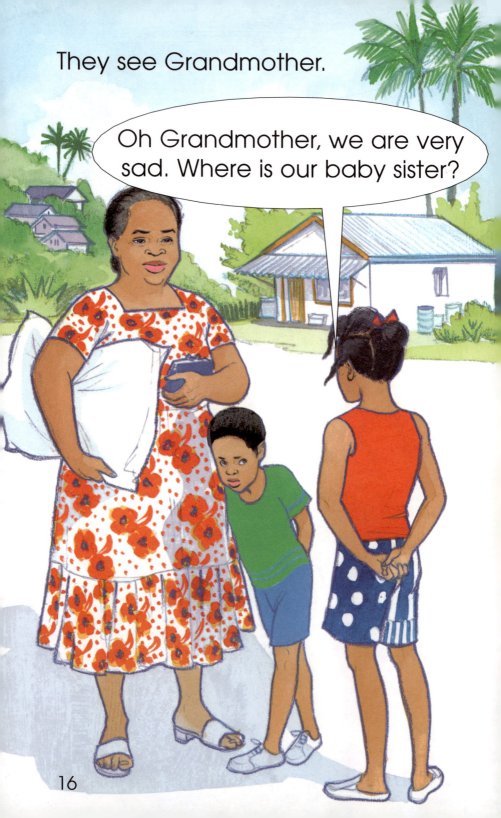

Alice, Sam and Grandmother are at home now.

© Copyright text Shelley Davidow 1998, 1999
© Copyright illustrations Macmillan Education Ltd 1998, 1999

All rights reserved. No reproduction, copy or transmission of this publication may be made without written permission.

No paragraph of this publication may be reproduced, copied or transmitted save with written permission or in accordance with the provisions of the Copyright, Designs and Patents Act 1988, or under the terms of any licence permitting limited copying issued by the Copyright Licensing Agency, 90 Tottenham Court Road, London W1P 9HE.

Any person who does any unauthorised act in relation to this publication may be liable to criminal prosecution and civil claims for damages.

First published 1998
This edition published 1999 by
MACMILLAN EDUCATION LTD
London and Basingstoke
Companies and representatives throughout the world

ISBN 0-333-77063-3

10 9 8 7 6 5 4 3 2 1
08 07 06 05 04 03 02 01 00 99

This book is printed on paper suitable for recycling and made from fully managed and sustained forest sources.

Typeset by Tek-Art, Croydon, Surrey

Colour Separation by Tenon & Polert Colour Scanning Ltd.

Printed In Hong Kong

A catalogue record for this book is available from the British Library.

Illustrations by Maureen and Gordon Gray